THE PITTSBURGH PENGUINS

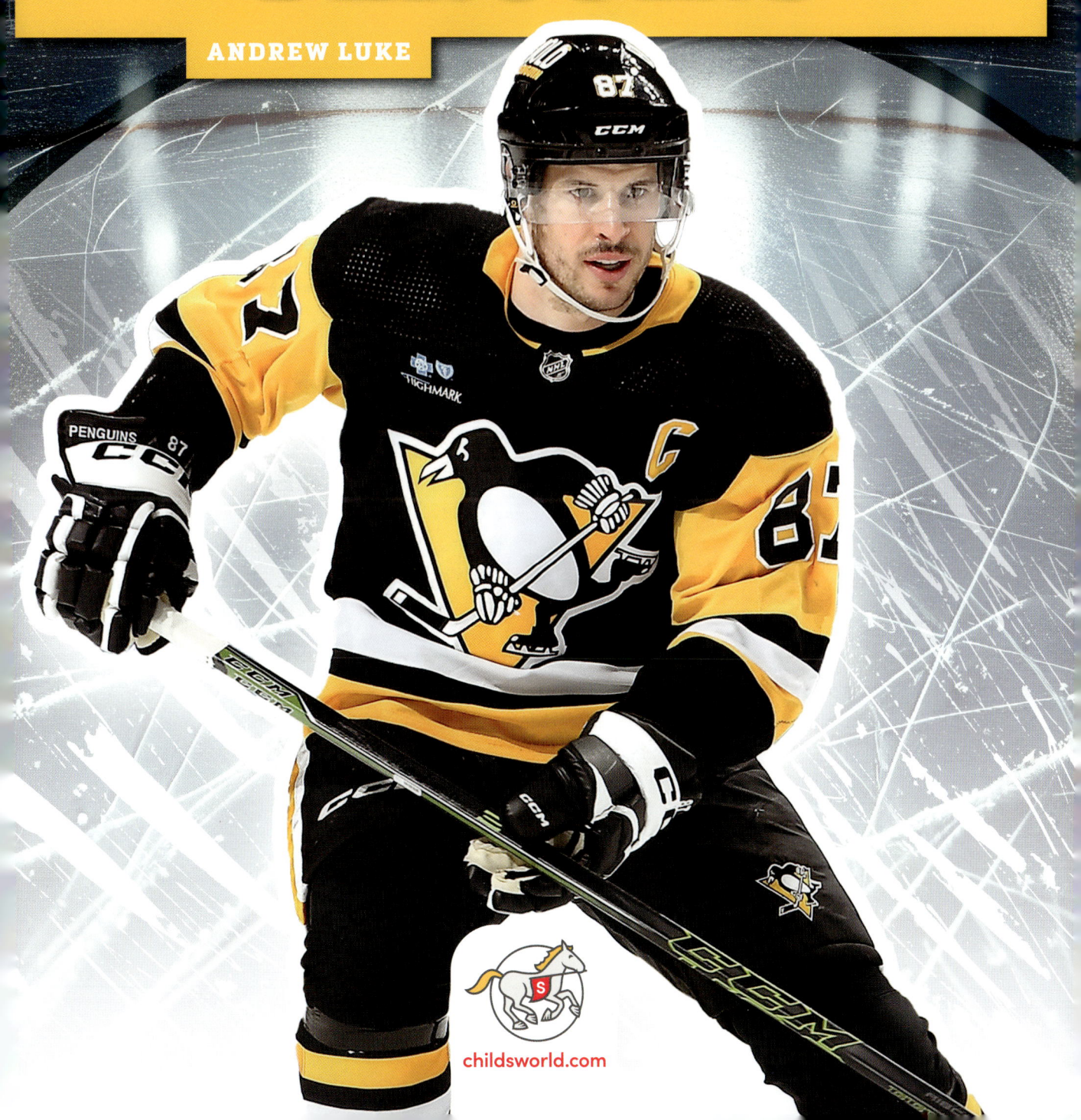

ANDREW LUKE

childsworld.com

Published by The Child's World®
800-599-READ • www.childsworld.com

Copyright © 2026 by The Child's World®
All rights reserved. No part of this book may be reproduced or utilized in any form or by any means without written permission from the publisher.

Photography Credits
Cover: ©Joe Sargent/NHLI/Getty Images; multiple pages: ©Hanna Siamashka/iStock/Getty Images; GLYPHstock/iStock/Getty Images; md tauhidul/Shutterstock; page 5: ©Justin Berl/Getty Images; page 6: ©Denis Brodeur/NHLI/Getty Images; page 9: ©Gregory Shamus/NHLI/Getty Images; page 10: ©Emilee Chinn/Getty Images; page 12: ©Joe Sargent/NHLI/Getty Images; page 12: ©Minas Panagiotakis/Getty Images; page 13: ©Joe Sargent/NHLI/Getty Images; page 13: ©UPI/Bettmann Archive/Getty Images; page 14: ©Justin Berl/Getty Images; page 16: ©Melchior DiGiacomo/Getty Images; page 16: ©Denis Brodeur/NHLI/Getty Images; page 17: ©B Bennett/Bruce Bennett Studios via Getty Images Studios/Getty Images; page 17: ©Bruce Bennett Studios via Getty Images Studios/Getty Images; page 18: ©Bruce Bennett Studios via Getty Images Studios/Getty Images; page 18: ©Bruce Bennett Studios via Getty Images Studios/Getty Images; page 19: ©Dave Sandford/Getty Images for NHL/Getty Images; page 19: ©Bruce Bennett/Getty Images: page 20: ©Joe Sargent/NHLI/Getty Images; page 20: ©Joe Sargent/NHLI/Getty Images; page 21: ©Joe Sargent/NHLI/Getty Images; page 21: ©Joe Sargent/NHLI/Getty Images; page 22: ©Eliot J. Schechter/Getty Images; page 23: ©Steve Babineau/Allsport/Getty Images; page 25: ©Bruce Bennett/Getty Images; page 26: ©Focus on Sport/Getty Images; page 29: ©Denis Brodeur/NHLI/Getty Images

ISBN Information
9781503870741 (Reinforced Library Binding)
9781503871946 (Portable Document Format)
9781503873186 (Online Multi-user eBook)
9781503874428 (Electronic Publication)

LCCN
Library of Congress Control Number: 2024950382

Printed in the United States of America

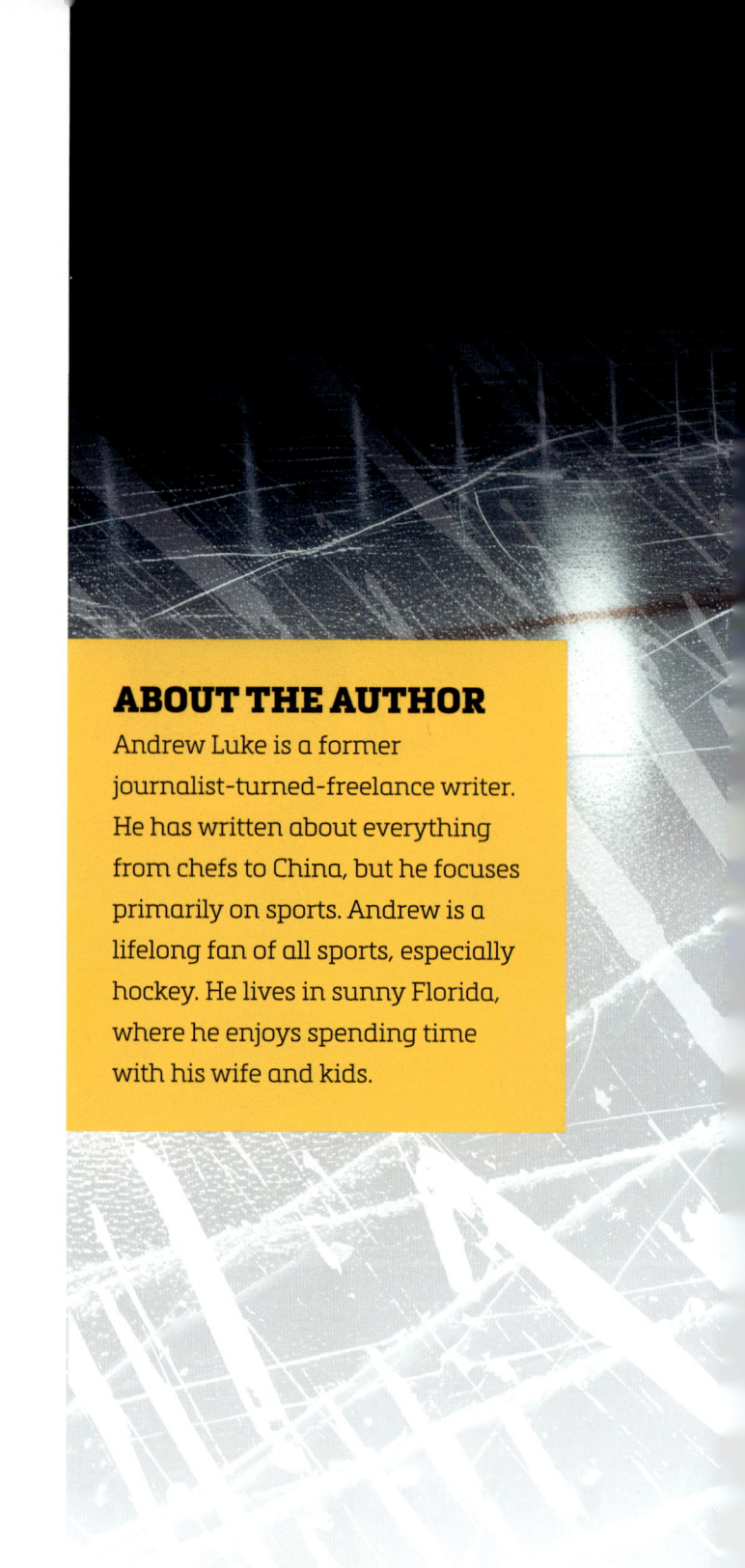

ABOUT THE AUTHOR

Andrew Luke is a former journalist-turned-freelance writer. He has written about everything from chefs to China, but he focuses primarily on sports. Andrew is a lifelong fan of all sports, especially hockey. He lives in sunny Florida, where he enjoys spending time with his wife and kids.

CONTENTS

Go Penguins! . . . 4
Becoming the Penguins . . . 7
By the Numbers . . . 8
Game Night . . . 11
Uniforms . . . 12
Team Spirit . . . 15
Heroes of History . . . 16
Big Days . . . 18
Modern-Day Marvels . . . 20
The G.O.A.T. . . . 23
The Big Game . . . 24
Amazing Feats . . . 27
All-Time Best . . . 28

Glossary . . . 30
Fast Facts . . . 31
One Stride Further . . . 31
Find Out More . . . 32
Index . . . 32

Go Penguins!

The Pittsburgh Penguins play in the National Hockey League's (NHL) Metropolitan Division. The Metro's first season was 2013–2014, and the Penguins won the division. The team is known as the Pens to their fans. They have two main division **rivals**. The Washington Capitals are their biggest rival. They also have a rivalry with the league's other Pennsylvania team, the Philadelphia Flyers. Whenever the Pens play the Caps or the Flyers, the game is usually sold out. Let's learn more about the Pittsburgh Penguins!

Eastern Conference • Metropolitan Division

Carolina Hurricanes	**New Jersey Devils**	**New York Rangers**	**Pittsburgh Penguins**
Columbus Blue Jackets	**New York Islanders**	**Philadelphia Flyers**	**Washington Capitals**

The Penguins celebrate a 2024 win over the Columbus Blue Jackets.

Les Binkley was the Penguins' first starting goalie.
He played on the team from 1967 until 1972.

Becoming the Penguins

The Penguins joined the NHL in 1967. That was the season that the NHL doubled the number of teams in the league. One division included the Original Six teams. These are the Toronto Maple Leafs, the Montreal Canadiens, the Chicago Blackhawks, the Boston Bruins, the Detroit Red Wings, and the New York Rangers. The second division had six new teams. New teams that are added to the league are known as **expansion** teams. These teams were in Pittsburgh, Philadelphia, St. Louis, and Los Angeles. The division also included the California Seals and the Minnesota North Stars. These two teams no longer exist. The Seals no longer exist, and the North Stars moved to Dallas, Texas, in 1993.

Pittsburgh has had two **dynasty** periods. The Pens won back-to-back Stanley Cups in 1991 and 1992 behind Mario Lemieux (pronounced luh-MYOO). They repeated this feat 24 years later, when center Sidney Crosby led Pittsburgh to Cup wins in 2016 and 2017.

By the Numbers

Mario Lemieux and Sidney Crosby have put up huge numbers in their careers with Pittsburgh. Here are some other interesting number facts about the Pens:

14 — The Penguins sold out every home game for 14-straight seasons, from February 2007 to October 2021. That streak spanned 633 games!

17 — The 1992–1993 Penguins set an NHL record when they won 17 games in a row.

5 — All five of Pittsburgh's Stanley Cups were won on the road. They have yet to win the Cup in front of their home fans.

21 — Sidney Crosby was just 21 years old when he led Pittsburgh to their third Stanley Cup win. Crosby is the youngest captain ever to lift the Cup.

Sidney Crosby and the Penguins defeated the Detroit Red Wings in seven games to win the 2009 Stanley Cup.

8

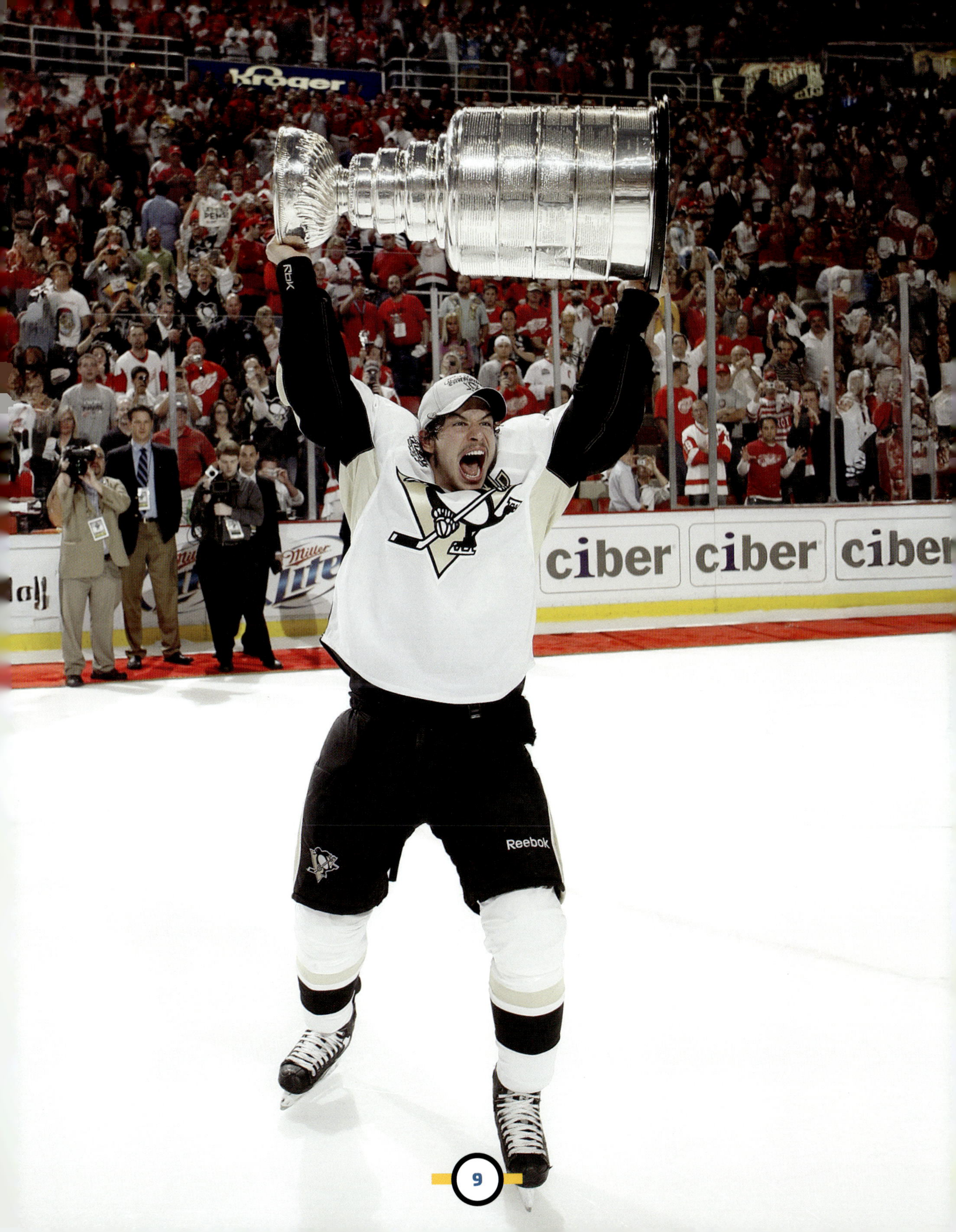
Kroger
ciber
ciber
Reebok

The Penguins helped pay for PPG Paints Arena, where they have played home games since 2010.

Game Night

The Penguins played their first 42 seasons at the Civic Arena. It could hold about 17,000 people. It was a white building with a domed ceiling that was nicknamed "The Igloo" because of its shape. The Civic Arena closed in 2010, and it was knocked down in 2012. The Pens moved across the street to what is now PPG Paints Arena. The brand-new arena holds more than 18,000 Pens fans. A goal horn that was originally in Civic Arena plays before games and whenever the Pens score.

We're Famous!

In 1993, the hip-hop group A Tribe Called Quest released their album *Midnight Marauders*. The album featured the song "Keep It Rollin'." One of the song's famous lyrics is sung by Phife Dawg and goes, "Large Professor in the house, you know how we do. I skate on your crew like Mario Lemieux."

Uniforms

HOME

AWAY

Sentimental Tribute

Hockey goalies paint their masks to express themselves and share their personalities. During goalie Marc-André Fleury's last season with Pittsburgh in 2016–2017, the Penguins were scheduled to play in the Stadium Series. This series includes a special regular-season game played outdoors, usually in a baseball or football stadium. Fleury had a mask specially designed for the event. It honored several of the teammates he had played with since the Pens picked him first overall in the 2003 NHL **Draft**.

Truly Weird

When the Penguins joined the NHL in the 1967–1968 expansion season, the team mascot was a penguin. No, not a guy in a penguin suit—an actual live penguin. The bird was a Humboldt penguin from Ecuador named Penguin Pete. He was loaned to the team for home games by the Pittsburgh Zoo. Pete got sick and passed away just a few weeks into Pittsburgh's second season. He was replaced by another penguin called Re-Pete.

14

Team Spirit

The Pens gave up on using live penguins as mascots after the 1971–1972 season. Pittsburgh went without an official mascot for 20 years. That changed when the team introduced a new mascot in 1992. This time, the Penguins went the traditional route and put a guy in a penguin suit. The giant penguin mascot is named Iceburgh. The name is a clever combination of the words *iceberg* and *Pittsburgh*. He entertains fans at PPG Paints Arena for all 41 home games each season.

◀ Iceburgh spends most of his time at PPG Paints Arena, but he also visits local schools and hospitals in the Pittsburgh area on his days off.

Heroes of History

Jean Pronovost
Right Wing | 1968–1978

Jean Pronovost played right wing for the Penguins for 10 years starting in 1968. He scored at least 40 goals in four of those 10 seasons. This includes 52 goals and 104 points in 1975–1976. Pronovost and teammate Pierre Larouche were the first Penguins to top 50 and 100 in those categories. Pronovost played in four **All-Star** games. He was tough and reliable, never playing in fewer than 66 games in a full season. Pronovost was voted into the Penguins Hall of Fame in 1992.

Jaromír Jágr
Right Wing | 1990–2001

Jaromír Jágr played a whopping 24 NHL seasons, 11 of them with Pittsburgh. The 10-time All-Star winger joined the Pens as a **rookie** to start the 1990–1991 season. He was a key player on the 1991 and 1992 Stanley Cup championship teams. He scored a playoff career-high 24 points in 1992. His 439 goals are the fourth-most in Penguins history. Jágr retired after 1,733 career games, which is fourth all-time in the NHL.

Ron Francis
Center | 1991–1998

Just behind Jágr on the all-time games played list is Ron Francis. He played in 1,731 games in his 23-year career. The four-time All-Star center was known for his ability to pass the puck. His 1,249 career assists rank second all-time behind only Wayne Gretzky. In 1991, Pittsburgh traded with the Hartford Whalers to get Francis. He joined the team for its Cup run that season and was a key team member when the Pens won again in 1992.

Marc-André Fleury
Goaltender | 2003–2017

Pittsburgh picked Marc-André Fleury first overall in the 2003 NHL Draft. It is rare for goaltenders to be number one draft picks. Fleury is one of only three goalies to be chosen with the first pick in NHL history. It turned out to be a great pick. Fleury played the first 13 of his 23 NHL seasons with the Pens. He was on three of their Stanley Cup championship-winning teams. Fleury is Pittsburgh's all-time leader in wins, with 375, and **shutouts**, with 44.

Big Days

JUNE 9, 1984

After a terrible 1983–1984 season that includes four separate six-game losing streaks, Pittsburgh gets to pick first in the 1984 NHL Draft. They choose Mario Lemieux.

Pittsburgh defeats the Minnesota North Stars 8–0 in Game 6 of the Stanley Cup Final. The win gives the team its first-ever championship.

MAY 25, 1991

JULY 30, 2005

With the first overall pick in the 2005 NHL Draft, Pittsburgh takes center Sidney Crosby. This is the key move in returning the team to greatness.

The Pens beat the Detroit Red Wings in seven games to win the first of three Stanley Cup championships under captain Sidney Crosby.

JUNE 12, 2009

Modern-Day Marvels

Sidney Crosby
Center | 2005–Present

Sidney Crosby, like Lemieux before him, is a **generational** player. Sid the Kid is not only one of the two best players in Penguins history, but he is also one of the 10 best players in the history of the NHL. The eight-time All-Star and two-time league Most Valuable Player (MVP) has led the league in scoring twice. Crosby is also a two-time playoffs MVP. He won the first of his two league scoring titles in just his second season. Crosby became the youngest team captain in NHL history at that time. He got the job at just 19 years old.

Evgeni Malkin
Center | 2006–Present

Evgeni "Geno" Malkin joined the Penguins in 2006, one year after the team drafted Sidney Crosby. The two centers have played their entire careers together in Pittsburgh. In Malkin's first six seasons, the three-time All-Star won Rookie of the Year, had three 100-point seasons, led the NHL in scoring twice, and was named league MVP. When Malkin won the first of his three Stanley Cups in 2009, he was chosen as the playoffs' MVP.

Joel Blomqvist
Goaltender | 2024–Present

Finnish goalie Joel Blomqvist may not have been the Pens' starting goalie in his first season with the team, but he is still considered one of the team's best young players. Drafted in 2020, Blomqvist played several seasons in the **minor league** before getting a shot with the main team. When Blomqvist posted an outstanding .921 save percentage with his minor league team in the 2023–2024 season, the Pens knew he was ready for the NHL. They hope he will be their goalie of the future for years to come.

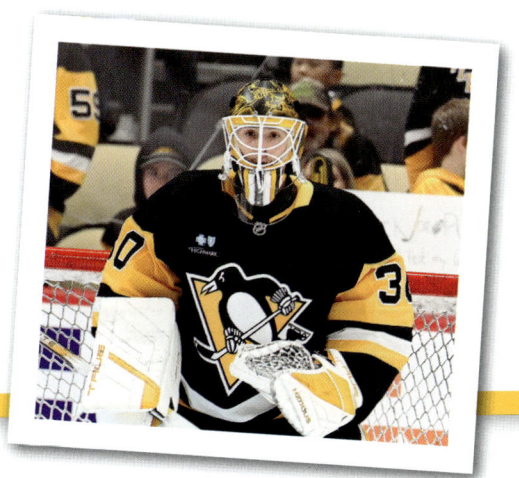

Kris Letang
Defenseman | 2006–Present

Pittsburgh drafted Kris Letang the same year as Crosby, just 61 picks later. Along with Crosby and Malkin, Letang has been a core player for the Penguins for nearly 20 years. Letang is known more for his offense than his defense. He has had seven seasons with 50 or more points. The two-time All-Star has struggled with health issues. Letang won an award as "the player best exemplifying perseverance, sportsmanship, and dedication to hockey" when he returned to play after a career-threatening illness in 2022–2023.

Many sports fans and experts consider Mario Lemieux the best ever to play in the NHL.

The G.O.A.T.

Mario Lemieux is not only the best player the Penguins have ever had. "Super Mario" is one of the top five players in NHL history. Lemieux scored 1,723 points in just 915 career games. That's an average of almost two points a game! The nine-time All-Star won three league MVP awards in 17 seasons. He never played a full season due to injury and illness. Despite this, he racked up 10 seasons with 100 or more points. Lemieux also led the league in scoring six times, which only two other players have ever done.

Fan Favorite

Martin Straka was a small player known for his big heart and determination. The Penguins drafted the winger from the Czech Republic in 1992. In his 10 total seasons as a Pen, Straka scored 442 points in 560 career games. His **overtime** goal against the Washington Capitals in the 2001 playoffs is an all-time Pens highlight. Straka was a hardworking player on both offense and defense, and the fans loved him for it.

The Big Game

In 2008, the Penguins and the Detroit Red Wings were two of the best teams in hockey. They faced off in the Stanley Cup Final. Detroit won to claim its 11th Cup in team history. The next season, the teams met again in the Final. The 2009 series went back and forth. It came down to a must-win Game 7 in Detroit on June 12, 2009. The hero of the game was not Crosby or Malkin. Instead, second-**line** center Maxime Talbot scored two quick goals halfway into the game, and the Pens hung on to win 2–1 to claim their third Stanley Cup.

Maxime Talbot scored eight goals during the 2009 playoffs compared to Sidney Crosby's 15, but the two he scored in Game 7 were the most memorable.

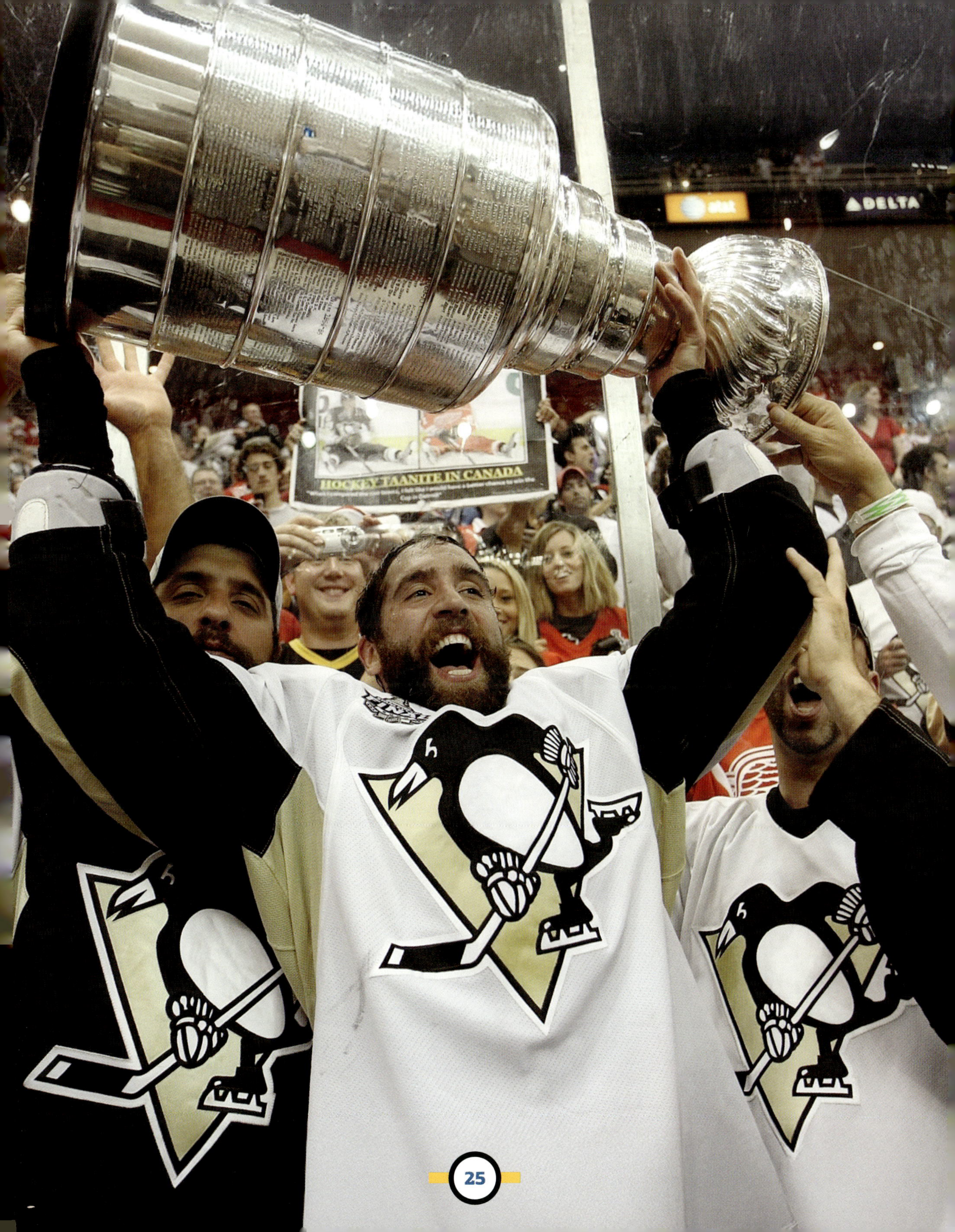
DELTA

Mario Lemieux scored 85 goals and handed out 114 assists in the 1988–1989 season.

Amazing Feats

Shutouts
In 2014–2015, Penguins goalie Marc-André Fleury posted 10 shutouts to break Tom Barrasso's previous record of seven shutouts in a single season.

10

Goals
Penguins Hall of Famer Paul Coffey holds the team record for single-season goals scored by a defenseman. Coffey scored a team record of 30 goals in 1988–1989.

30

Scoring Streak
Sidney Crosby has averaged at least one point per game in a record 19 seasons in a row. The only other player ever to do this is Wayne Gretzky.

19

Points
Wayne Gretzky is the only player in NHL history to score 200 or more points in a season, but Mario Lemieux came as close as possible in 1988–1989 with 199.

199

All-Time Best

MOST POINTS
1	Mario Lemieux	1,723
2	Sidney Crosby*	1,636
3	Evgeni Malkin*	1,327
4	Jaromír Jágr	1,079
5	Kris Letang*	758

MOST GOALS
1	Mario Lemieux	690
2	Sidney Crosby*	602
3	Evgeni Malkin*	506
4	Jaromír Jágr	439
5	Jean Pronovost	316

MOST ASSISTS
1	Sidney Crosby*	1,034
2	Mario Lemieux	1,033
3	Evgeni Malkin*	821
4	Jaromír Jágr	640
5	Kris Letang*	585

MOST HAT TRICKS
1	Mario Lemieux	40
2	Sidney Crosby*	13
3	Evgeni Malkin*	13
4	Kevin Stevens	10
5	Jaromír Jágr	9

MOST WINS
1	Marc-André Fleury	375
2	Tom Barrasso	226
3	Tristan Jarry*	144
4	Matt Murray	117
5	Ken Wregget	104

LOWEST GOALS AGAINST AVERAGE
1	Marc-André Fleury	258
2	Matt Murray	267
3	Tristan Jarry*	275
4	Casey DeSmith	281
5	Johan Hedberg	286

*stats accurate through December 2024

Jaromír Jágr is the oldest player in NHL history to record a hat trick—he scored one at age 42!

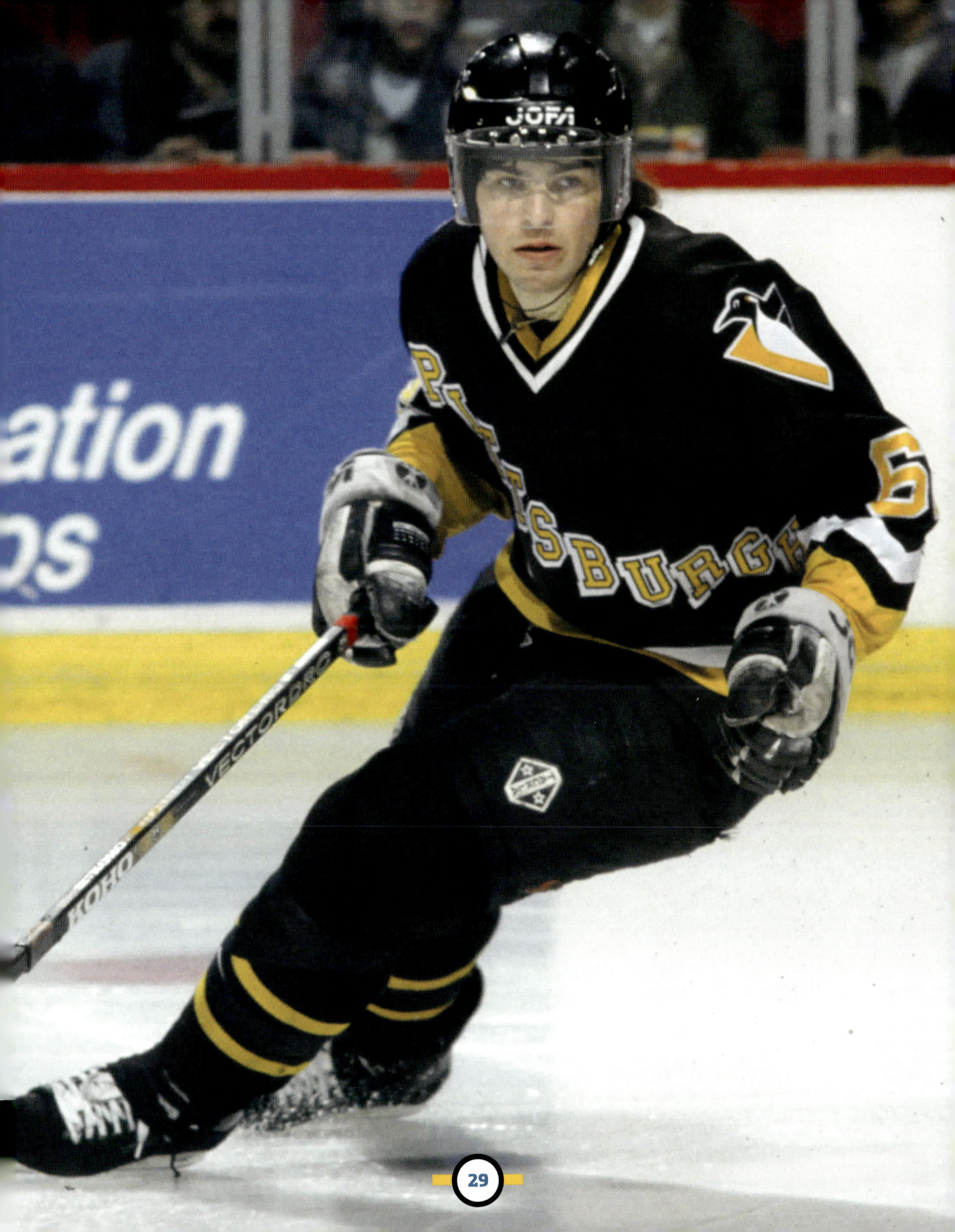
JOFA
ation
VECTORPRO
KOHO

GLOSSARY

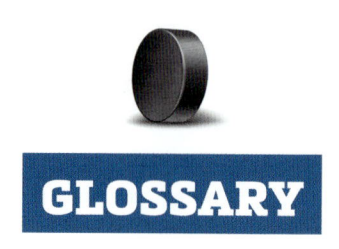

All-Star (ALL STAR) An All-Star is a player chosen as one of the best in their sport.

draft (DRAFT) A draft is a yearly event when teams take turns choosing new players. In the NHL, teams can select North American ice hockey players between the ages of 18 and 20 and international players between 18 and 21 to join the league.

dynasty (DY-nuh-stee) A dynasty is a powerful group, such as a team, that leads or rules for a long period of time.

expansion (ex-SPAN-shun) Expansion occurs when the league adds new teams to its membership.

generational (jen-er-RAY-shun-ul) Generational describes an athlete who is so dominant that their level of play is only seen once in a generation.

line (LYN) A line in hockey is made up of a center, left winger, and right winger who are on the ice at the same time.

minor league (MY-nor LEEG) The minor league is a professional league that is below a sport's top league. Young players often start in a minor league to gain valuable playing experience.

overtime (OH-vur-tym) Overtime is extra time added to the end of a game when the regular time is up and the score is tied.

penalty minutes (PEN-ul-tee MIN-uhts) In hockey, penalty minutes or PIM is the total amount of time a player spends off the ice for committing fouls.

rival (RYE-vuhl) A rival is a team's top competitor, which they try to outdo and play better than each season.

rookie (ROOK-ee) A rookie is a new or first-year player in a professional sport.

shutout (SHUT-owt) A shutout occurs when a goalie keeps the other team from scoring any goals.

FAST FACTS

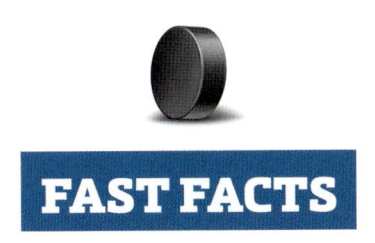

- The Penguins' colors switched to black and gold in 1980 to match the colors of the city's other pro teams—baseball's Pirates and football's Steelers.

- Mike Sullivan has racked up more than 375 wins as the most-winning coach in team history.

- Evgeni Malkin is the team's all-time leader in **penalty minutes** (PIM). As of December 2024, Malkin has spent 1,176 minutes in the penalty box.

- Mario Lemieux retired from the NHL—twice! He first retired in 1997 due to injuries, but made a comeback in 2000 and played five more seasons. Lemieux retired for good in 2006 at 40 years old.

ONE STRIDE FURTHER

- Mario Lemieux and Sidney Crosby played one season together before Super Mario passed the torch to Sid the Kid. Find other situations where an all-time great player was immediately followed by another superstar and give a detailed report of how that transition went.

- Which championship do you think is the hardest to win: the Stanley Cup, the World Series, the Super Bowl, or the NBA Final? Make a list of reasons to support your answer.

- Ask friends and family members to name their favorite sport to watch and their favorite sport to play. Keep track and make a graph to see which sports are the most popular.

FIND OUT MORE

IN THE LIBRARY

Anderson, Josh. *Sidney Crosby vs. Wayne Gretzky: Who Would Win?* Minneapolis, MN: Lerner Publications, 2024.

Association of Gentlemen Pittsburgh Journalists. *Pittsburgh's Civic Arena: Stories from the Igloo.* Charleston, SC: History Press, 2021.

Druzin, Randi. *Behind the Mask: A Revealing Look at Twelve of the Greatest Goalies in Hockey History.* Vancouver, BC: Greystone Books, 2023.

Kelley, K.C. *Connor McDavid vs. Mario Lemieux: Who Would Win?* Minneapolis, MN: Lerner Publications, 2024.

ON THE WEB

Visit our website for links about the Pittsburgh Penguins:
childsworld.com/links

Note to Parents, Caregivers, Teachers, and Librarians: We routinely verify our web links to make sure they are safe and active sites. So encourage your readers to check them out!

INDEX

Blomqvist, Joel 21

Crosby, Sidney 7–8, 19–21, 24, 27–28, 31

Fleury, Mark-André 13, 17, 27–28

Francis, Ron 17

Iceburgh 15

Jágr, Jaromír 16–17, 28

Lemieux, Mario 7–8, 11, 18, 20, 22–23, 26–28, 31

Letang, Kris 21, 28

Metropolitan Division 4

PPG Paints Arena 10–11, 15

Pronovost, Jean 16, 28

Stanley Cup 7–8, 16–20, 24, 31

Straka, Martin 23